Rouge

J.R. ROGUE

Rouge

Limited print run - 1st Edition.

2nd Edition can be found at createspace.com

$7 /200

ALSO BY J.R. ROGUE

La Douleur Exquise
Burning Muses
Tell Me Where It Hurts
An Open Suitcase & New Blue Tears

COMING SOON

Le Chant Des Sirénes
Background Music

Dear Reader,

In late 2014, I created an Instagram account to share my writing with the world. It was at once both thrilling and terrifying, but I never looked back. Writing is my therapy. I need to get out the manic words that bounce around in my head or I'll lose my mind (what's left of it). Finding others in this world who connect with your sorrows, soar with your achievements, and devour your soul is an indescribable feeling. Within these pages, you will find many of my social media follower's favorite pieces and the first words I shared with the world. We are always growing, always moving forward. I am constantly fascinated by the many women I meet living inside of me. It is necessary and humbling to look back at our small, simple first steps.

I don't regret a bit of this journey.

These words are red and real.

They are rouge.

Thank you for trusting me.

Thank you for listening to every part of my story.

she was rouge
and red lips

dark hair and
soft hips

mischief and laughter

she wanted you to love
her faster

it's getting harder to
do this with you

you still wear that smile,
you still listen

I just wish you
had something
to say

perhaps it's time
to put this old
photo away

- moving on

Rouge

I have been dreaming
more and more each night

and some mornings
my dreams are
sleeping next
to me

how I smile at their
warm breath
     on my neck

- *you are my dream*

          I'm sorry I make
            love stories
           out of crimson,
         scraps, and lust

           they are the tales
         I need to tell myself

     when this day turns to dusk

- *fairy tales for my fears*

I don't want forever,
no, I just want you to
devour me

just for a night,
leave me
speechless,
breathless,
and worn

I'll find my voice again,
and I'll let them see how beautiful
we humans can
~~sometimes~~
        be

- my voice

I wasn't sure why
I was drawn to him

he was pure and good

I wanted to bathe in
his marrow
and hope some
of this sin
of mine
would wash off

- to bathe in you would be beautiful

patience has never come
easy to me,
I want what I want,
I want it now
                no delay

if you h e s i t a t e for a second
I will move on to my next obsession

I don't want that with you

I want to wait,
I want to be steady and unmoving in
my affections

you are worth more
than I can write

and the part that kills me is
that you can't see it

- I can be your mirror

please, steal my pen,
steal my words

I'm only trying to write
us as a tragedy,
because those
are the tales I take to
most

- bad habits

we drank
and we laughed
and we cried
and we twisted ourselves
around each other in
the sheets once more

it was goodbye,
but we made it
beautiful

- goodbye

I am beyond terrified,
I am fear

I feel its film all
      over my flesh

he is coming at me
with honest affections

and my palm is rested
on his chest

the dull
thud of his intentions
beats with my own
resistance

- fear

the boys I loved best?
I ran from them
because I knew
they would follow

then I would turn and
face them head-on
with an open palm
and a martyr heart

I wanted to see if they
would only fall to my
feet if they tasted
my retreat

love me,
not the
chase

– the chase

his candor was
intoxicating

I always filtered my words
and
he let them fall in
torrential truths

I laughed
and I let myself out
in strange ways beneath him

strange to me,
strange to that bed

it doesn't have to be complicated

he was
fun and
so
was I

— *uncomplicate your life*

Rouge

I let my heart out,
I was all feathers and fairy tales
for a fraction of a second

fear not,

I've found my favorite cage
                          for her

- my cage

                              give me a man
                        with a sharp closet,
                            a soft tongue,
                        and the ability
                            to kill me
                                with
                                both

                    - tell me it's you

I love my face with a bit of color

after a day working on
those stubborn hedges
in front of my little yellow house

after a quick run

after a stranger compliments
      me out of the blue

after he presses
his steady tongue
against that spot
between my inviting thighs

- *color*

my face looks ridiculous
as if I slept with a coat hanger
in my mouth

that high I feel won't
last long

his frenzied fuckery
nearly made
me late
for work,
and I left
my give-a-damns
on the
kitchen counter
again

it's amazing how a new
lover can erase your
memory for half a day

- *fuckery*

I wonder who she is—
the woman
walking around with
his one-of-a-kind
specific key slipped snuggly
into her back pocket

I wonder if she
knows the door
it will slip soundly into

if she knows
the curve of his neck
and the feel
of his skin beneath her own

I wonder if he has yet
to meet her

I wonder how long I will
be standing here
turning the knob
with no one on the other side

- I can not stop this loving you

please, don't tell me
you're falling for me

don't make me wait for
the moment you've landed

keep that secret so
very very secret

I'll be hanging on
every word
every touch
every press of your lips

I'll be waiting,
as you're changing
your mind, as you're telling
yourself new secrets

that it was never love
that it was just infatuation
that I'll never know
if you just slip out the door,
out of my life
so very very silently

- stop the lie

let's stop playing the game,
let's stop stacking the deck

we add as many potential lovers
to our lives as we can
(oftentimes repeats from the past)

odds are someone
will end up wanting us,
odds are we will lose the one
we wanted most
when they learn just how special
they really were not

- the times we live in

I am torn apart,
my heart is cracked

both sides say
your name,
they just
say it in different
ways

- they both love you

I can't help but cry
at our petty fights,
our simple arguments

they all bring tears

the smallest crack
can bring down the
strongest foundation

and though castles have
always fascinated me,
they're nothing more

than the ruins
of lives
lost

- let us not be in ruins

baby,
please love me
in something more
than bar
            lighting

- my plea

you're switchblade
sarcasm,
shy smiles, and
sex,

and I'm insatiable

- you are sex

hearts are broken every damn day

you're breaking mine
and somehow I'm
still breaking his
and on
and
on
it
  g
    o
      e
        s

- the cycle

I want to hear
every word you say
and understand
all the ones you
          couldn't

- listen

we could be the
perfect pair,
the real he
and the
fictional me

- masks

you'll have that,
the days you remember
the raw and
breathless kisses

and though you
never exchanged
those three words,

in hindsight,
your love for them was real

and despite
the how
and why
of your parting,

you may see
now,
they knew it too

– *a small solace*

I have more in this
mind than I'll ever be
able to tell,

please read my
sighs and
downcast
       eyes

- read me

         each day that I
lose more and more
of this mind
of mine,

I hope to be finding
my heart

- my lost heart ♥

Rouge

I've got scars
stapled to thin skin
and a sad soul

so silly of me
to assume
you'd
see something
            sacred

- silly me

                              with you,
                    there is no plateau

                    & I've always been
                    terrified of heights

                    - boundless you

will we all lose ourselves
to comfort?

we crave it,
but it cripples us

we'll trade in our passion
and regret,
that's
what good little
grown-ups do

we will die a little more
each day,
and we will find
sick comfort in it

- sit back and relax

I can never again let myself
fall for a man who will not shed
tears with me

no, not to a man
who believes the definition
of masculinity is written
with taciturn words
and bold letters that
feel nothing,
taste of hardened hearts,
and shy away from the
many tender things
in this world

feel the earth move with me,
listen to her whisper
between our clasped hands
and our newly kissed lips
and our unkempt hair

feel everything with me
and I will never ever
have a reason to leave
this unmade bed

– *redefine beautiful masculinity*

I am the curious kind
    of places
    of religions
    of history
    of languages
    of the way beautiful
        men look under their clothes

- there is beauty everywhere

everyone loves
me with a buzz
I am wild,
open, careless, free

and the boys,
I won't kiss them
unless I have two or three

but every 'next morning'
I find myself talking
to the ceiling saying,
she wasn't me

- will the real me please stand up?

swipe left
    then left
        then left
           then left
then throw in a right,
take another sip, and
                drug the night

it's faces and not true love and that's
fine because the other
is magical unicorn
shit and you know,
you're not a little girl anymore

let's kiss the fairy tale goodbye
and kiss a stranger

let's forget that the rattle
of your broken parts
clanging and clashing together
inside is too maddening
to escape

– 21st century dating

I'll let you
undress me,
but this
loneliness,

I'll always wear

- little black loneliness

It's been so long since I've
fallen into anything other
than this dark

since I've been exposed

I don't let myself

because the only
thing that will hold
me is
this ache

- there has to be more

Rouge

I wish you had an interest
in my form, the way you did last night

but you seem to have
your eyes on that box in the corner
not me

I've filled out nicely
I was a frail thing before, turning away love
and a decent meal,
preferring solitude and ignoring hunger
not just that of my heart

I wish you would notice, but you're already
starting to go the way of the last,

you don't care about my form
my soft curves and
suddenly new and softened heart

you care about that box in the corner,
the one you would like to put me in
    you'll hold me back just as my last
                      lover

- I am not what they want me to be

do you want to know
which words are for you?

when my soul is bound and
sold, will you wonder
as you turn each page?

there are pieces of my past
pieces of pure fantasy
pieces of you

just run your hands along the
ones that move you,
                    where you feel me

run your fingers along
            this
                    page

- you are here

don't tell me how strong you are
that won't break me down

show me your stamina
show me sixteen months from now,
sixteen years

show me
         us
your ear placed at
        the hollow between
           my breasts
a tear on my cheek,
slowly
    surrendering yet
        another fragment

- surrender

vulnerability has
never come easy to me

yet here I am pouring myself
onto a page, day after day,
and even worse, showing the world

if you were to ask me about it
face to face
I would smile a little
and maybe throw a laugh in there

oh, it's mostly made up bullshit

I can't be confronted
with pity pupils and *I'm sorry* smiles

I retreat inward,
I pull up my shields

it's something I wish
I didn't have to do

- help me release

you say I need help
a good doctor and some pills

I'm broke, I know
not just inside,
    my wallet's too dry

so, dear, if you
won't pay the bills
I'll just be here with my pen
and a dollar-store pad of paper
working my
    way through the black

- *cheap therapy*

    this rope holding me to you is strong,
        it's burning me
        it's choking me
        it's breaking me

    alas, there is no one else I'd rather
        have holding the noose

- *only you*

I want to end your life,
this life you know

slight highs
and dank, gray-toned lows

save a spot for me
among the deeds you
deem as sins

I'll play the role well

I want you to end my life,
this life I know,
with you so far away

- I miss you

he's not the kind of man
to stay out late drinking,
the kind who leaves me
        worrying
           and
               wondering
with mysterious texts to
unknown numbers

he's not the kind of man
to play silly games,
to seek revenge for the
times my passive-aggressive
ways have wounded him

– he's the kind that stays

we all have that one,
the person who lives
within our bones

that heart-wrenching
unrequited love

the one who gives
you the taste of their skin
but nothing more

I was not immune

I had him,
the one I compared all others to

I broke their hearts
for the shadow of him on my wall

I am not special
I admit, I was a fool
I do not know why, one day,
he decided to love me too

- hamartia

I believe in more
because of him

that you can stop thinking
about your feelings
and
instead
      just feel them

that it
can be real,
despite
expectations
and the
grim
   grip this world
            has on
                  you

- *expectations are the enemy*

call it fleeting
call it a passing fancy
call it whatever you want
hell, I don't know what to call it
call it my salvation
call it my resurrection
call it the day I finally breathed fresh air
call the day I found him whatever you like
I will not name it, I will not define it
it defines me

- nameless

I have lost my edge
I was always on top
I always won the silly games
that were played for
lust and love and dominance

maybe I've just grown up
maybe I've just become more wise
maybe love has finally beaten me

- you win, love

she has this smirk,
              it can wound

I feel a thrill when it cuts the air,
and it was always followed by
a remark cut from the same edge

I think of her on cobalt and crimson days,
when I miss the way she
would cry a little
alone
on her pull-out bed

then plot revenge in a
tent made of sheets at 2 a.m.

I wish she loved me the way I love her

she must have crossed out my name,
her to-do list was ever long

I miss the old me

– *cobalt and crimson*

I am bouncing around between
wishing I never met you
and repeating your name
over and over in my
prayers to some deity with no face

nothing really makes
sense now without
you in my future

nothing really makes
sense now that my life
is one of those novels women curse because
the two lovers they invested
in, never got together after all

I'm bouncing around between
believing in soulmates
and settling for some sad suburban
house neatly
laid in
a row

- settling down with the wrong one

you always loved in past tense
so beautifully

I always felt a jealous jolt
ripple through me
when you spoke of the women
from before

the ones who had
ripped apart your heart

so I left,
         and it was easy

now I am as adored
by you
as they always seemed
            to be

- we are fools, no?

his love for me feels weightless
and taupe in color

like it never was a love at all

I'm learning to cope
beneath the sway
and pull of others
                    he's just caught up in
                    the thrill of it all, I said

and I still see it as truth

he waits for me to change
my mind
and knows,
as I do,
that I never will

- taupe

he's gentle and too
forgiving

I imagine
the women in his
past saw it as clearly
as I do

an easy target
for their deceit-dipped
arrows

all I really
want is for him to let
        me love him
to show
him how fucking
beautiful he is

to show him
I will not hurt him
as the last did

- he loves the hurt more than he loves me

I am not defined by who loves me,
I am defined by love
 the love I have inside
 despite circumstance
 despite my marital status
 despite what I write on
   that damn tax form
 despite the ones who left
 despite it all

- I am love

     he's a pusher
    a gentle pusher
  he pushes these notions into me
    that I can love myself
    that I can pat myself on
    the back from time to time
    that I am beautiful and I am
    brilliant and I am desired
    for more than this skin
    I walk around in

- he's a pusher

43

this bar is a harbor,
so I'll dock my soul for a night

you know I'm looking for you,
most moons
you do not show

don't worry, I'll take a shot for you
and wait for you to
drift back
          too

- I will wait

                    there's a solace in
                        finding others
                who share your demons,
                    hide their memories,
          find comfort in your words

                    but mostly there is
                          sadness

- double-edged

promise me you'll whisper dirty nothings
and somethings to me in my
hotel room and make me feel pure again
under those city lights

promise me we can forget
everything our names, our burdens, our lives apart
for just a few days

promise me it will be like the last
moments we shared,
                promise me it will be more

- *promise me*

              I promise I won't be timid the next time

       I promise I'll tell you every little spot to press

              I promise I'll give in to your skin and
                        forget what we can never be

              I promise I will come easily

                  - *and I promise you*

his love for me
does not waver
despite everything I put him through

he stands still,
quiet

I am ready to stop
throwing the
              dark at him

- his beautiful constance

If you promise to
let me travel this world
until I grow weary of it,

I will promise to
live
forever

- wanderlove

I romance you
and
you
regret me

long-term love,
it isn't easy
at times

it's messy
it's scary
it's sad

and at times you
fall out of love

only to fall back
that much harder

- we will come back to each other

I'm sorry I'm the match

I'm sorry you're
the tinder

- the fire between us

give me a reason
to play

I've been wound up too tightly
for too long

convince me
with your lips,
with your
fingertips

I'll call in
for the day
just a day

and we'll explore
long forgotten
thrills
together

- never forget to play

I spent too many years
trying to land a man
to put a diamond ring
on my hand

a man to help me
pop out a little
brown-haired mini-me

because that's
all anyone wants from me

I spent too many years
chasing

not enough
paying attention
to what I really want

– broken blueprints

it always comes down
to Christmas

to empty-boxed dreams
and frightening glitter

it always comes down
to me
with a one-way ticket
to anywhere
clutched in my left hand

and yours dropping
from my
right

- I am sorry, I must go

loving me is war,
the only
survivors
have been
deserters,
cowards

but
free of me
is something I know
you long to be

- the coward survives this story

I was the brightest
light he
had ever seen

and he loved
turning me
on

- luminosity

I've always been
told I am
too intimidating to approach,

and it's strange to me
that they can't see
how soft my heart is

- soft heart

my lover loves me
to him, it is
                    more
I feel the same
but I dare not say it
I dare not let him in on the secret

my lover loves me
and he has forever
clutched in his
architect hands
            he builds me up
he saw my ruin
and looked back
with skyscraper eyes

- the secret

I'm having a hard time sleeping,
or maybe sleep is
having a
hard time
having me

- insomnolence

eat a poet's heart,

and satiate that
hunger
    for humanity

- devour me, dear

I still don't quite yet
know who I really am

and that excites me

- the journey

Rouge

I have a temper,
and I'm nearly impossible to take
most days

please, don't love me

I want to save you from
every scar my past lovers
wear

and I do love your skin
just the way it is

- the warning they never hear

I was never very
good at breaking
hearts

I'd rather step
on my own

for a clear view
              of your smile

- *you are the one to break me*

                      my tears remind me
              that this world of ours has not
                  yet turned me to stone

              - *we weep, we live*

Rouge

I need someone
to kiss the tender
side of my wrist

I need someone
to touch me without
the promise of getting off
(and hey, they rarely
care if I do)

I need someone
to need me
for the calm
my palms can bring

I need someone
to help me feel a little less

seams are stretched,
there is this pressure
building

I need someone,
I need someone
to need me

- need

every time another
ex gets down on
one knee,

I feel an entire small
town
frowning at me

-their expectations

I'm wrapped up
with worry
and weary wants

and I just wish to
wander back to you
and the warmth you would
always wind back
into my wounds

- your warmth

too often, we want to play the part of a one-
dimensional woman who never gets upset

we let shitty things happen to us in the beginning
and choke on our true feelings

because, what if we say how
we really feel and then end up back on
that dating website we thought we left behind?

we accept mediocrity,
we accept a lack of respect and behavior we
ourselves would never put anyone through

why can't we just let our true selves out right
away? isn't that the part of us that needs to be
loved?

and yes, I am guilty of this every damn time,
I am no better

I wish in the beginning
I could find no fear in being naked
and exposed in anything other
than a physical way

— *mediocre men*

we don't buy each
other fancy gifts

I told him not to bother,
long ago

the things I need from him
aren't tangible

he offers them
to me
freely

I feel them everywhere

- he gives me what I truly need

right now,
I have this overwhelming
urge to run

from him
from life
from anything that makes me smile

one word flashes in my mind
over and over

I've always been good
at fucking up my own life,
and old habits
            are kissing me tenderly

- sabotage

imitation castles and sweat-stained backs,
that's my April Saturday
I'm playing make-believe and
feeling all too real

I'm in this skin,
d   e   e   p   e   r   than I've ever been
able to go

I chose myself and I'm begging,
between panting breaths,
as I climb this
Ozark hillside,
to not break my own heart

the sky can't be closer
and I can't be more
present than
             I am now

I'm always going to be that girl
    the one who wears a brand
    new shirt to the party
    with the tag
    accidentally still attached

the girl who never checks
    the weather so she'll
    always steal your coat

the girl who can never say goodbye
    so you'll just have
    to let her go

- that girl

all I've ever wanted, all I'll ever desire
is the kind of lover who wants to stand
at the edge of a cliff and scream my name
proudly at the world

he will know I am
his, just as I am my own

- I belong to myself first

I am a blade

and I keep falling
all over myself

Rouge

I remembered today
what it was like to
play on a merry-go-round
as a child

it would spin so fast,
round and round,
and I would hang on,
white-knuckled,
alive

I thought of us today too

I guess falling for you
was the same kind of thrill

dangerous,
but I held on,
white-knuckled,
alive

- you spin me

let's stay in tonight
leave your work troubles,
expectations,
and clothes at the door
     it's raining, and finally,
     I'm not crying

I'll open the window and read some
of Sylvia's secrets

you can read the bruises you left
all over my smooth skin
and remind me
which rooms we
     made love in

- bruises

     text me in the middle of the day
     make me smile, make me blush

     please don't make me wait

- the little things

Rouge

all I could see
were roses
and the retreating sun,
it
set everything
on fire

your touch,
as I carefully
removed my dress,
and my resolve

burned longer
than the lingering rays

leaving us to dance
with the late
July shadows

- the night I fell for you

it's in still moments
when you lie still
on your side,

when I
trace
the tattoos
on your skin,

that I
I feel our
connection

- still

inside of me
is but a fragment
of every person
I have met,
loved,
hurt,
touched,

and lost

each one of them
has something
to say

- are you listening?

I can hear retreating steps
before the first
footfall

I can taste my bad decisions
before I've had the
chance to say grace

- premonitions

he always dressed
in black

as to hide my
ink-stained fingerprints

from other
lovers

- his tricks

it wasn't in the arms of another,
it wasn't with lies or deceit,
it wasn't with goodbye

I broke his heart by fooling myself
into believing I could be everything
he needed

- too much bend

sometimes
the lover in our lives
who will hurt us the most

is the one who
is looking back
from the mirror

- I, Villain

I need moments
often
to be alone with
the murky mania
of my mind

I'll come back,
just give me
these moments

- alone with the dark

she doesn't want
the safe bet –
    my heart

it's all she's known

I'm weary of shells
and ducktape stitching

let me out
    let me in
        let me be yours
I won't run

fit your fingertips
around my nape

tell me everything
and say nothing

– I am listening

Rouge

I've never tried drugs
I've never felt the need

with the way
my heart stops and starts
in the moments
before your lips
meet mine,

why would I look for
thrills elsewhere?

- you are a drug

lately I feel
like love
has little to do
with
who will
last

- and it saddens me

I love myself enough
to know
that reaching
for you
as you reach for the
door
is no
longer enough

- self love

those things you fear
will eventually catch you

you just have to figure out
how to face them

when running is no
longer an option

- you've got this

I'm not into fast cars,
fast talkers, or fast lovers

take
      your
           time
               with me

- we move too fast

I love sleeping
next to you,
and that's strange

I've never been one
to sleep with the
light on

- he is my light

as children we were
fascinated
by magic,
as adults we fear love

at what point
did we forget
they
are the same thing?

- love and magic

when did I
become
the kind of woman
who finds more
truth
in
interlaced fingers
than raveled limbs
and pressed lips?

- the truth lives in small moments

I think my heart escaped

I can feel it whispering
from all the places
I want your lips

- my pulse

I suppose you always knew
I hated goodbyes

you wouldn't let us
begin,

so we'll never have
an ending

- the trick

he's reserved
and I'm rolling in regret
for things said

but never
for things
felt

- risk and regret

our bed has a way of
twisting things for me

whether you're
here beside
me or not

I tangle myself in the
sheets and
shed every woe

all of our problems
fall away,
and I feel nothing
but my love
for you

I wish we
could spend forever
here

- our bed cures it all

I can count on
these fingers
all the reasons
we should
have ended
long ago

but
I'd rather use
them to
touch you

- to touch you is to love you

I find myself smiling,
the small kind,
at the thought
of your
skin against mine
somewhere in
our next life

- redux

this heart,
I fear,
is a burial ground

the kind you
dare not
visit at night

full of restless
memories
and hands

you're always
reckless
enough to hold
them

- your reckless abandon

I was taught this world
is round,

yet I always find myself
breaking on
her sharp
edges

Rouge

lips and fingertips
     exploring, imploring,
     he was never ignoring

the woman beneath
     the skin as soft
     as her beating song

picking up slowly
     beneath the warm
     water spray
     and tentative
     attention

- beating song

how you take
broken pieces
and make a whole
woman
out of me,

I'll never know

- your gift

walls upon walls
of books fill our home

still
the only words
he longs to read
are the ones

caged within my heart

- I am the story he needs

he left me for another,
it's a tale that's
been told time
and time again

he left me for the memory of
who I once was

he'd rather live with
her than this monster
I have become

- the other woman

happiness scares them,
the foolish boys
you gave your heart to

so you play
it cool,
it's a game you
plan to win

but you lost the
moment
you let them
convince you
laughter should be hidden

and not caught
with
their own
smiling lips

- this is how they win

I love my good days
    when my demons
    are sleeping,
    away

when the dusk of one
    kisses the next's dawn

I love the way he looks at me,
I love the way he lies
    and we pretend it
        never has to end

- my good days

I've never had much balance in my life,
except the night I held steady
on that barstool in
my kitchenette

as you gripped my hips
and tore my new
lace

- new lace

there's something inside of me
that I hide

      not just my truth
      my scars
      my past

there's something inside of me
      dark,
      that I like
      that I miss

that wants to play

all I want is to be
beautifully broken

so please,
overuse me
like that phrase

- clichés

did you waste
your worth
throwing pennies
down the
wrong wishing
well?

we will all worry,
we will all wait
for the day we wind
up where
we are wanted

- wasted worth

ask me why
I love you again

I'd love to shut you up
for a while

— lip service

fall in love with
yourself
when you can

you're going
to spend the
rest of your life
together anyways

— you can love yourself today

sometimes
they don't break
your heart by leaving

sometimes they
break your heart
by staying

sometimes you
break your heart
by staying

- complacent

I think I figured out
today
what peace is,
if only
for a fleeting moment

I held it with my hands,
and you held back

- you are my peace

I wonder if
we are the kind
who can
outrun the
tragic paper trail
of our past

— let's run away

give me less than perfect
give me something
broken in his eyes
give me someone
looking for
salvation
in this fragile
woman's
arms

— give me the one who needs me

he loves to kiss me,
between our lips
we share tequila,
salt,
and fire

but I'm
never a sober
desire

Rouge

I'm just a girl
and I w a n t

I want four walls,
I want a warm embrace

sometimes it doesn't
matter who has their arms around me

I have a wild imagination,
I can pretend it is someone
who adores me

- let me pretend with you

kill me with your kiss
the kind I crave

I'll carve comfort
out of
your cruelty

- your killing kiss

J.R. ROGUE is very active on social media & encourages you to follow her around.

Instagram

https://www.instagram.com/j.r.rogue/

Facebook

https://www.facebook.com/jrrogueauthor/

Facebook user group

https://www.facebook.com/groups/
1627799237440695/

Twitter

https://twitter.com/jenR501

Website

www.jrrogue.com